Many Waters

fal

fal

Award-winning books from Cornwall

Dear Shadows	DM Thomas
Keeping House	Bill Mycock
Olga's Dreams	Victoria Field
Sleeping in the Rain	St Petrocs
Once in a Blue Moon	Angela Stoner
Seiriol and the Dragon	Michael Power
The Devil and the Floral Dance	DM Thomas

www.falpublications.co.uk

Many Waters

Victoria Field

fal

First edition 2006

ISBN 10: 0-9544980-7-0
ISBN 13: 978-0-9544980-7-8

Published by

Fal Publications
PO Box 74
Truro
TR1 1XS

www.falpublications.co.uk

Printed by

R. Booth Ltd
Antron Hill
Mabe, Cornwall

For Ian Sherwood, priest, friend and lover of Byzantium

Contents

Acknowledgements

I would first like to thank the Dean and Chapter, the cathedral staff and the whole community in and around Truro Cathedral who have unfailingly made me feel welcome during this residency.

I would also like to thank those who have helped shape some of these poems; including Zeeba Ansari, Dominic Power, Penelope Shuttle, DM Thomas and George Wallace and, for their support for my writing, Les Murray and Christopher Rush.

Some of these poems, some in earlier versions, have appeared in the following print or online publications: *Cornish World, Quadrant (Australia), Poetry Bay, the Poly.* The author gratefully acknowledges the support of these publications and their editors.

'December' won second prize in the Lanlivery Churchtown poetry competition, 'November' was Commended in the Bill Winter Award 2006, 'Doing Theology' and 'Shades' were long-listed in the Virginia Warbey Poetry Prize 2006 and 'And Martha Served' was in the final ten of the Manchester Cathedral Religious Poetry Competition 2006.

Foreword

Victoria Field was appointed Artist in Residence at Truro Cathedral at the beginning of Advent 2005. Truro Cathedral exists to proclaim the glory of God through its worship, prayer, and mission. It is a place of beauty, holiness, music, art, peace, architectural wonder, and spaciousness, where those of every tradition and none can come and experience something of the love of God. Victoria has used the Residency as a means of genuine reflection and dialogue with the Cathedral community, and in this new collection of poems, 'Many Waters', she encourages the reader to engage with 'Cathedral life' creatively and questioningly.

These poems are immensely enjoyable and also challenging and insightful. Victoria skilfully develops the role of the arts in the interpretation of the Cathedral and I have no hesitation in commending this collection to you.

Christopher Hardwick
Dean

Threshold

Heavy doors sway
batting warm air and cold
this way and that
through the days of our lives.

Our hands rest
where a thousand palms
have pressed before us –
pushing towards whatever awaits.

We are always leaving
one place, arriving in another,
moving in and out of ourselves
to and from the things of the world.

Winter; the porch is cool,
full of ghosts of these comings
and goings – you heading one way,
me in the other.

The Day

when sadness
rolled around
the house in coils
of wet grey

when gloom slid
through the sashes
and cracks
under the doors

touching everything
with cold fingers
undulating
pages of books

filling logs with fog
so kindling
wouldn't take
the chimney

stopped breathing
laundry collapsed
on the line
there was no way

of knowing
field from roof
tree from earth
death from life
in the grey of that day.

Gifts of the Women of Truro

Diligence of small stitches
Precision of folded sheets
Uplift of well-risen sponges
Radiance of polished brass
Purity of whites on the line
Clarity of swept floors
Patience of stacked plates
Timeliness of flowers
Open-heartedness of lace
And tired, worn hands that say
We love this place.

December Walk

On the shortest day, I read the birds
Starlings massed on black trees
are hieroglyphs telling the loss of the sun

Blackbird grammar
clatters from chaos of brambles –
warning signs written in sharp tongues

High, dense clouds –
a lower-case lesson in how grey
changes imperceptibly,

stays always the same,
sky's flat repetition
of its periodic sentence

Lanes are books of choices –
chapters can't be re-read
with the knowledge of crossroads yet to come

The buzzard's
specialist subject is killing –
he's rehearsing bullet point answers to vole

Pheasants illuminate the fields –
too many colours on one page
tales of beauty, vulnerable

Some instruction surprises the starlings
they spill from scratched branches
like burning paper, fall on the sky

There's nothing to read in these lanes
but birds – puddles are clear glass
I am unwritten

On the longest night
moon rises in a curtainless window –
my wordless index of days.

A Woman Who Looks on Glass

In the last year of her life
she blew an unexpected legacy
on a vast picture window
for Cedarwood, the bungalow
where they celebrated
not quite sixty years of marriage,
sat watching Blackie and the other birds
diving for fat, nuts and cake, looking
for the old man in blue overalls
leaning on his rake in the lettuce lines
who wouldn't be in for his tea.

Climbing Down To Pednvounder Beach

We're being birthed in reverse
through a *vagina dentata*

of huge, smooth slabs
awry on green gums.

There are steep lips
but no tongue to tell us

of the *hortus conclusus*
gated by watery shifts

holding light below
in a shell-shape of sand.

Descent is trusting
to falling and breathing

Bone, skin and rock
become one

knowing only the edge –
the being between

the everything
that's not air nor Cornwall

nor granite nor water
nor now – all history
the tiny relief
of a footprint on sand.

January

January crosses
the threshold

closes the window
bolts the door.

January looked
both ways

and said
No more.

Last year's ashes
fill the grate

January says
Too late –
too late.

Sleeping Out

Above, no ceiling, light bulb, lamp or shade
Below, no sheet, no mattress, no carpet on the floor
Beside, no table, books, no pouring of a pot of tea
In front, no door, no stair, no window pane

Around, no papered, patterned or painted walls
No pictures, drawers nor wardrobe, no change of clothes
No roof, no kitchen, no fire, no chair, no warmth
No locks, no table, no kettle, no things at all

What's left is air and sky and ground and cold
And stars and moon and dark, freezing toes
And aching bones and heavy hearts that plead with those
Who are rushing home, not to let the day grow old

Without a thought for those we don't hear weep or shout
The fragile, silent dreams of those who are sleeping out.

Doing Theology

Take your question, hoist her
up on to your knee,
tell her bright and terrible

stories of scripture – show her the feeding
of the five thousand, the felling of Goliath,
Mary's amazing hair, watch Daniel's angel

calming lions – see where she smiles or frowns,
when she sleeps through the darkness
or wakes from her nightmares –

watch your question express whatever runs
through her – how she dances, sings,
fasts, paints on the cave's empty walls

Lead her in and out of churches
Does she like candles, incense, choirs? How
does your question pray – on her knees

in a bare chapel on a cliff? Tying ribbons
to a tree by a well or perhaps only once
in her entire life, finding thickened flesh in one breast?

Throw questions to your question, see
how she returns them, back to the centre
of your racquet or way out

beyond your boundaries
Let your question follow you
like the small dog who always knows

exactly where you are, take her to shops
the pub, the park, wait in hospitals
browse a library, visit a tiny school on the moor

She'll spot those feeding the hungry
show you where the answer is –
she can smell it a mile off

Take your answer, put her on your knee –
tell her the bright and terrible stories of scripture.

Lent

February dreams
of an improbable spring

where all the hens of the world
yield their hoarded eggs

held in hollows of old trees
and she makes

pancakes from five thousand
yolks, filling her kitchen

with the yellow smiles
of Lent lilies,

beats whites into stiff starched
gowns for angels

a bright shroud
to be left behind in a cave –

in her dream no one is hungry
the gorse and the may

can't wait to be part of it all
but the sun's uncertain

born too soon, shivers like a wet lamb –
February – not quite beautiful

wakes in a field
white with sudden snow –

she's a once much-wanted guest
who doesn't understand it's time to go.

Sob Story

This man is neither scruffy, nor smart, not eager to talk
Not shy either, not bearded, not quite clean shaven.

Must be a lovely place to work. My reply, *It is*.
He waits. *Are you visiting?* Hesitates. *Sort of.*

I look encouraging. Mistake? Says he came looking for a cliff
high enough to end it all. Found himself in Newquay. Then

due to his rare genetic disorder, was taken to the local hospital,
diagnosed with a mini-stroke and, now, he's here, hoping for the
      answer.

Has he found it? Not yet, it's comforting – looks up, around
      – but there's
the worry of whether to spend the night on the street or get the
      bus

to Plymouth and hang out there, although his house (all paid
      for), credit cards,
money, farewell notes for all his mates are far away in
      Harrogate.

Thirty eight with the heart of an eighty year old – eighty year
      old hearts
don't last long. He'd travelled the world but not seen Cornwall,
      took control

headed here to end it all – sister, same rare disorder, is on
        holiday,
Mauritius, Seychelles, somewhere warm, could have gone too
        but instead

came here. Parents died when he was just fifteen, father cancer,
        mum
half an hour later of a heart attack from shock. Only nine
        pounds in his pocket,

no ID – everything at home, didn't think it would be needed,
        see. Feels hungry
now he's thinking of living. Do I know anywhere cheap to eat?
        Would

they give him a train ticket for free if they knew the story? Not
        that
he's desperate or anything but it's cold. I rack my brains for
        where to send him.

Advice comes free but I have no clue. His need is crystal clear
        and he's asking me.
He was eight last time he wept and his father said *No man in this
        house cries.*

And beat him with his belt. I believe that's true.

Writing Workshop

The tools couldn't be simpler,
pen, paper, table, chair

Add history, heart and mind –
it couldn't be more complex

Build small cathedrals on paper
from the sigh of the out-breath,

the vibrations of tongue on teeth.
Dig down to the sound of spade on rock

Brave scaffolds to build a spire
alive with flowers, try to touch the sky

Be methodical, weigh words
before use, choose your stones with care

Granite with its secret sparkle
or those more beloved

when they crumble, willingly weaken
to time and wear. Be brave, knowing it can be done

That everything began with a single
Word. See the cathedrals

multiply, simple and complex
as the lilies in bud massed in their buckets

waiting for Easter, each lovelier
for being side by side with the others –

Seeing light for the first time
over and over again.

Asleep

One day, I was sleeping in
when I saw a thread begin
to make its way along the wide ceiling

a thin crack crawling from corner
to corner, the small beginning of disaster.
I was far away, lost in my dreams

when plaster began to flicker
down to me – the opening grew wider –
still I slept – until great chunks like teeth

fell to the bed, waking me, made me look up
beneath the gaping rafters – but before
my thoughts could ravel, the roof took flight.

I lay in my bed beneath the unforgiving sky
not knowing whether to pray or cry
when fate suddenly, with his sleight of hand

whipped the sheet and bed from under me –
the whole house too, that was once a home
left me clutching just a blanket and a carrier bag,

my address that night, the old, cold ground –
nowhere to go, nowhere to hide
from voices saying I brought it on myself-

no point in saying there was once a house
with a roof between me and faceless stars.
How it happened's hard to say.

I was asleep one night
and didn't see the crack begin.
I didn't know it would grow

so huge I'd be left alone
ignored, bereft of home –
sleeping out and looking in.

Ye also ought to wash one another's feet

This cathedral is a show of hands instilling
hope into candles, tilting the chalice,
receiving the soft press of the host,
rows of palms open like flowers for rain

Hands tell of the weather, hang
in sad laps, hold a head heavy and clouded
with thought, gently hush the lips of a joyful child
creating her very own echo. They seek those

of strangers for peace, grieve a lost love's touch
then join their faithful partner in prayer.
But feet carried us here with our burdens
of being, their fret of small bones untouched, unseeing,

remembering how, once, they might have been washed
and wiped by the towel wherewith He was girded.

Good Friday

It was night
the horizon
swallowed
the sun

It was night
rainbows
turned grey –
painters wept

It was night
the moon
showed
her fickle face

It was night
thieves took
joy
from that place

Stars stayed
far away –
and someone slept.

And Martha Served

They made a supper
and it was I who served
Lazarus, of course, was there
but it was I who served

I watched him, warm with life
among those chosen men –
I'd swept clean the room
and arranged the chairs

It was I who served and I
like things neat, the plate
and cup within our Saviour's
easy reach, everything

just so. I brought the bread
soft and white as flesh
and dark, warm wine
that poured both deep and slow –

it was I who served –
a shadow who was barely there
while she let loose her waves
of wild hair and perfumed

the room with something
strange and sweet, daring –
as I would never do –
to wash his dear, unblemished feet

I'm barely seen as I tidy, serve
and clean, ignored and empty
as the air. It was I who served
Yes, I was there.

Votive Candles

There are Candle Days
    when supplies run out
    over and over again –
    it's hard to keep up –
    filling buckets with empties
    after such long parties of prayer.

The waiting candles
    are constellations of moons
    patient wafers at the Eucharist
    bright faces of babies
    frozen ponds, not yet skated on
    dreaming of heat.

Full of commitment
    as relay-runners,
    each lit candle's a baton,
    a passing on,
    both gift and a burden.

Like daisies in a chain
            they hold memories
            of summer days
            slow moments
            in long summer grass.

The flames are private
            like our thoughts this long night,
            the warmth rising invisibly
            with your last breath
            still there when the light has gone.

Spent wax forgets about whiteness,
            it's wet glass – not quite clear,
            leaving empty, cups without promise,
            a spilling of coins, silver on sand,
            longings, elsewhere.

If it die, it bringeth forth much fruit

See how, as a golden grain
a spinning sycamore seed
a tight, bound bulb
I am perfect

There are worlds
hidden within me
all is potential, possibility
forests and fields

I like being whole
and singular, my skin
tight around my smallness
at ease in my dry sleep

I fear entering the earth
the chink of cold spade
the damp heft of its weight
above, below, around

I fear the rain
breaking me open like tears
the green shoots of spring
fusing through me

If I grow, I know
I will disappear
be spent in the earth's night, my husk
succouring fruit that isn't me

Can I bear to be broken open
by life's longing for itself
let love die in the darkness
to live again in the light?

Contact

Blue eyes in a pale face
mouth struggling
he's had a stroke, I think
the words tangle in effort
eventually I get it
he always comes here for ...
priest ... peace ... play ...?
from his carrier bag
he pulls a paper bag
from the cathedral shop
shows me a card with a verse about
oh – prayer
he's bought four of these cards
for his friends
in Plymouth – no
Birmingham – no
somewhere
I understand
he's pleased to meet me
we shake hands
he drops the cards
they slide around us on the floor
we laugh, gather them up
his eyes are bluer than any Cornish blue
I can't quite meet them
they are speaking to me
telling me something
way, way beyond words

Somebody's Clothes

At first, she wore her life unthinkingly,
the garment that just came to hand
before she knew what hands were,
fitting her snug as a peach she could

still grow into; then others began to borrow
and wear bits of her, not always lightly,
losing a button or two, busting a zip
so her lovely life faded, bagged at the elbows

still wearable, though, til something
finally snagged and the thread holding it
all together unravelled, leaving
only a rag for a dipstick, wardrobe

emptied for Oxfam and the huge
undarnable hole she finally fell through.

As The Latter And Former Rain

Unexpected girls sway into the choir stalls,
their various gaits invoking birds or horses,

arranging limbs and faces like flowers in a vase
letting loose the colours of their voices,

coming into bloom as they become themselves.
They're the former rain, my own teenage tears

as today I walk drenched in the latter,
midlife storminess born of experience,

joy at their distant beauty. Their voices fill
my dark day with bright promises of spring –

then they leave, happily, swishing their little
skirts, innocent and knowing as the daffodils.

Blue Spot

The East Window watches us
with her one blue eye.

her beauty is blighted,
more than a mote –

flat, in a field of living colour
a bland reproach.

Early mornings and her false gaze
travels over God's people.

Of course it shouldn't be there.
But it is and we are –

blemished, wounded, damaged
faulty, wonky, wrong –

the grey in our hair, loosened flesh
beams in our own eyes, regrets

offered as evidence of lives fully lived,
His earth more than visited.

Human Lines

I've stood in human lines in churches the world over –
with ambassadors and refugees, queued to kiss icons,
engaged in the simultaneous standing and walking that is living.
Today at the head of this line – an old woman bent and slow.
A man stands by, ready, holding out his hand;
he smiles gravely, then decorously, as if they're dancing
at a strange and holy ball, helps her up one granite step
and the next, closer to the invisible curtain between us and
eternity.
We follow. Some human lines I've seen only on tv;
queues for rationed bread, women batting flies
from a baby's sticky eyes where something human
like hope, has already died – or long lines to vote
where elections aren't yet met with ironic detachment –
a woman creating her cross, remembering the iron taste
of blood on teeth. There are lines I don't understand
although I know they are human too – congas at weddings,
for sales at Next, entry to football games. I like the way
this human line forms here every single day, how we shuffle
forward to the light, move hesitantly through our own lives,
becoming a line of hands and mouths, fan out into our futures
of flesh and blood, after being, for one moment, truly one body.

Third Sunday after Easter

The end of April is yellow and white –
earth all three-cornered garlic and celandines.

The beginning of May is white and yellow –
every hillside clouded by blackthorn and gorse.

The end of April is walls of scent, doors open
silently into summer. The beginning of May

is carpets of sea, windows to wide horizons
and gates ajar. Walking between these months

is a path balancing land and water, held
in the arms of new grass, always heading west.

Something's begun – white as new linen
yellow as remembered sun.

Echoes

The speechless ones
Cannot sing or pray
In the approved way
Their limbs and lips
Refusing to obey

Sometimes they scream
From the wheeled chairs
That are a kind of home –
The echo replies in kind
Reliable as stone

Saying,
Yes, you too are here
You are heard
Your song is understood
Amen

Stillbirth

Sun fell like a holy orange
when he entered the silk of her sea.

She was alarming and lovely
as a painting on velvet,

a universe of rising moons
and meteorites

igniting a life as red
and specific as Venus.

When, later, it slid from her
too soon,

the small box was too heavy
for its ashen freight of grief.

Not just beaches
but whole galaxies gone,

a cathedral shrunk
to a small room, lid shut tight

where she watches the last
of the half-spent candles,

lets day become night.

Peregrine

I'm faster than light and darker than night.
Mine is the tower, the belfry, the spire.

This building is mine, my cliff and my rock,
My mountain, my crag, my dizzying drop.

Mine is the power, mine are the wings,
Mine is the choir, mine are the kings.

Nothing will ever bring me to my knees
As I circle and swoop and give no reprieve.

I'm an angel avenging for something unsaid,
Shock, awe for songbirds, primeval dread.

Life on the ledge, chasing through sky,
I am the one with the all-seeing eye.

Gravity's nothing, the heavens are mine.
See me circling, silent, and ask who's divine.

Rose

Exeter Station Cafe

I push the rose across the table.
make room for my coffee cup –

the pot's too light
floats in my fingers

I'm suddenly struck by false pink,
a plastic insult of leaves –

what seemed lovely, transitory
now tat, lasting for eternity

Then, I see globes of water
jewelled on its stem and soften

Once again, I love the rose,
reach to touch, taste wet on my finger

but learn instead of roses
Made in China,

of factory workers filling
the world with flowers

untrue but still blessed
with the dew of the new.

There At Our Waking

for Steve, Alyn and Robert

Door unlockers
Dust removers
Chair arrangers
Stonework hooverers

Direction givers
Drain unblockers
Time-to chatters
Smile elicitors

Secret keepers
Lectern polishers
History givers
Reasons to livers

Warmth providers
Time observers
Building dwellers
Bishop guiders

Limit knowers
Treasure carers
Service preparers
People readers

Child comforters
Big key turners
Cathedral fabric
and heart repairers.

Lucy

for her baptism

A little girl whose name means light
And light's the moon, the stars and sun

The moon is silver on a far-off sea
A crescent whisper in a clouded sky

And moon is Lucy's smiles and tears
She'll wax and wane and laugh and cry

And move among her sister stars
All bright as Lucy's changing eyes, as small

And precious as a child whose smile
Lights up a room, warms it as the summer sun

Makes roses bud and blush and bloom
Then fade as stars and moon their courses run

All come together in a girl whose name means light
And light is love and love makes all light one.

Interrogating the Abyss

If there were no cathedral
Would light fall colourless into the ground?

If there were no cathedral
Would a forest of pillars stand naked under surprised sky?

If there were no cathedral
Would the breezes blow sand into the candles?

If there were no cathedral
Would quarries be full of untouched stone and tools lying
idle?

If there were no cathedral
Would birds perch on a wooden throne?

If there were no cathedral
Where would tourists go on wet August days?

If there were no cathedral
Would those waiting for buses or heavy with prayer

Wander streets, shops and cafes
Imagining what might have been there?

Rose Window

complex, folded in on herself
rose holds the dove
radiates from her rose-self
a floribunda of flame
flickering tongues of orange,
red then redness aflame
with orange again and again
and around them in flower
twelve angels in blue and red
red and blue, fly and spiral
from the wheel's whirl of rose
rising from the dove's wings –
the enclosed garden grows
flowers into apostles
set in the squares of their circles
while this rational rose
petalled and curved
spinning wheels of creation
fast cycles of earth, red days
of moon and slow rhythms of sun
holds twelve holy men spun
from her rose-centre
set alight by wings of cool white
forever aflame.

Wren

The wren is writing
on my summer silence

I search for words
while she has plenty and repeats them

insisting on being heard
I am so small
she says

over and over
in her small voice

yet I'm filling
your garden

with cathedrals
each cheep a brick

each grace note
mortar filling the floral air

just write it she says
over and over again

building her wall
of small sounds by my window.

The Crossing Place

Teenage boys sing in the summer cathedral;
their bodies growing too fast, they're exuberant,
rampant with life, callow and beautiful; voices
connecting earth to sky, inviting light to touch grass
through complicated canopies of leaves.
They're on the cusp, like the old lady today
whose hand floats, confused, over the sudden cat
in her lap, tracing a half-remembered melody
of illuminated comfort and warmth while words
fall away, yield silently like snow in the forest.
Her room is cold and her roots are growing
down into darkness, relieving her of knowledge.

Many Waters

The cathedral loves her three rivers
embraces them, sits where they meet.
Kenwyn and Allen come down
and hold her at their lowest, most seaward point –
the Truro stretches up to greet them.

The little ones tickle her toes, stream in
from the granite spine of her country.
She knows she's enhanced, seen
from the South, against
the Truro's soft wide green.

Its changing levels love her back
like a painter add mutable light
to mud, turn greys to dull silver
til the moon tips the tide –
lifts boats and birds towards her.

They rise high as they can
bringing with them the world
on the out-breath of inflow
the cathedral always there
where waters meet –
something these rivers know.

Jewelling the Chalice

We kneel like St Nectan at the waterfall,
our cup filling with ribbons of light,

shedding pearls which bounce at our feet.
One girl gives her ruby ring. It's not

a broken heart nor blood from her wounds
but a baby crying its first breath,

held firm in hands of worked gold.
She gives it to grow

roses in glass
to know heaven in stone.

A widow's tears are stars for lost ships.
Yielding her diamonds is a blessing

like dew, new and precise
on each leaf in the forest.

His undone watch is melted time
bells marking his passing and coming again

like good bees in late summer
making more than they take.

Treasure mined from our longing
shines best in the light where emeralds

stud cathedrals of trees, where we share
the cup over and over again

passing it through a thousand hands
the song of the robin
falling freely as rain.

The congregation of St Peters, Eaton Square, London gave their jewellery to
decorate a chalice as a gift to Truro Cathedral

Father

from a line by George Szirtes

My father carries me across a field.
How did you enter this field?
Foxily, through a hole in the hedge
Under cover of darkness and birds' nests.

My father carries me across a field.
What sort of field?
Tussocky, chaotic with cows,
Desire lines leading through brambles and gorse.

My father carries me across a field.
Are you too tired to walk?
I'm just a child who might go astray.
His strong arms hold me close to his heart.

My father carries me across a field.
Is he a farmer, your father?
No, he loves black earth, broad beans
Horses and beer, but the land isn't his.

My father carries me across a field.
And then?
He's opened a heavy gate and gone through
Disappeared down a deep lane among trees.

There's no one carrying me across a field.
Just a tweed cap, flat in my hands
Trailing scents of lost autumn days
And a faraway voice, calling the way.

Service

People piss in me, men mostly
but women too, sometimes, after the pub.

I'm part of the open road but going nowhere.
A marker on the songlines of life, I shelter

the forgotten who don't wear the armour
of a vehicle, those who don't know out-of-town shopping

parties in rural houses, spontaneous trips to the city.
I absorb the anxiety of the elderly, clutching

their carefully counted fare, embrace the weak
whose whole world is hospitals, new glasses,

bewildering benefits. Am glad to be of service
to the naked. Where else can kids go

for a smoke or a grope? I wait for the waiting
who always leave me, move on as soon as they can.

I love the caresses of sanctioned rain and snow
but can take, too, the drunk's vomit, used condoms,

a hundred worried dog-ends and not mind –
be a station on life's journey on a parallel road,

let the truly human pass through me.

Sunday

after Chagall (1954)

I took your lovely face
showed it to the moon
told her you were mine.
Was I too proud?

Moon entered you, made
you different every day –
circled you in black.
Should I have protected you?

My arms, hair and the crook
of my elbow cradle you
Here – hedgerow flowers
for thanks.
Was that wrong?

We're leaving Vitebsk
pitched roofs, flashing gold
of a belfry, aroma of black earth.
I can no longer make out
faces of friends in the fields.
Are you sad?

This flight is luminous.
Such colours hurt
but how I want them –
purple of Notre Dame
blood of the Seine and Tour Eiffel
sharp as a sword. Look! Look!

Your face is so still.
Your eyes so wide.
Half of you already retreats
from my lipsticked lips.

Have I gone too far?

Treen

Earth and sky dizzy with sunshine
us walking through purples and yellows
that inside would dismay the eyes
but here on the cliffs
dazzled us in the dying days of summer

the steps round the Minack treacherous
the beach too white too perfect green
sea clear as bells made of green glass
great swells sucking and swallowing swimmers
cliffs cathedrals of tumbling blocks
huge heavy high a Logan balancing rocking

the tent rippled all night then sudden silence
when the wind whispered too low for understanding
the storm broke its promise
only the regular moan of the buoy
sad as a human tagged like Prometheus
far out to sea and the next day brightness
wiped away by a fog into stillness
and wet air hanging over us

harvest festival at St Levan a cut glass priest
pretty her parishioners hearty with blonde
children an old man on sticks whose mother just
turned ninety nine – three fishes dancing for the saint
his name a contraction of Solomon his stone
a giant bit of fissured granite two buttocks
rude in the churchyard – old pews harvest fishes nets
boats built of twigs dahlias abundant some pots
of jam carrots with mud on and carrots with none

you no glasses squinting me not needing the large
print hymn book a Methodist guest preacher
his Cornishness rumbling through the church
its twin naves its double altar like us two
you slender fast and sleek one of his fast fish
a flash of white diving into green Treen sea
dense foliage at your groin your skin a light surprise
me slow timid as a seal seeing all those towers
of rocks above tall black chasms
with jammed boulders bridging them
the big sea shadowed

give thanks said the old farmer turned minister
for the plenty the tomatoes flowers and jam
the colour give thanks for the not having no longer
to lug huge baskets up the fields dotted
bright green with forgotten potatoes catching
their green from the sea surplus to the hundred tons
a week sent for crisps

oh I could watch you in the waves
til the Guernsey cows come silently
home along the lane by the campsite
hot breathed and not minding

it's the green of your eyes
and love for which I'm thankful
yes thank you thank you thank you –
trying to do something green
with this language that can't be done.

'In Former Times

....a verger might have needed to use his virge to keep back animals or an overenthusiastic crowd from the personage he was escorting or even to discipline unruly choristers.'

Today, the Palm Sunday
donkey walks sedately.
At the Service for Pets,
no dogs chase the cats.

These days, we'll refrain
from mobbing Elvis,
the Dean or the Bishop –
(although perhaps we'd like to)

Choristers file in
orderly as angels.
Thank goodness, now,
we're amenable, reasonable,
so self-restrained.

November

In November, the trees
are too big for the woods

In November, the woods
are too bare for the birds

In November, the birds
are too black for the moon

In November, the moon
is too sad for the earth

In November, the earth
is too hard and too cold

She laughs at the sky
You too will be old.

Five Windows

Here is the soul with five windows of life
These are the windows harbouring light
Light is the measure of love in your eyes
Your eyes are the green of the weed in the sea
The sea is stretched out like the cries of the gulls
The gulls are the kings of the town where I live
I live in your love like a seed in the earth
Earth is the dark and the warm and the wet
Wet is the prayer of the fish I could be
The fish is the sign that shelters my soul
My soul opens windows to sun, moon and sea
Sea eats the starlight, swallows it whole.

Shades

As you walked that winter day, did you see,
when clouds gave way to sun, your shadow come?
Were you happy then, going along with your small
strange twin, joined forever at your feet?

I see you share the cliff tops, the short, bright
day but as time runs out, he, slow at first
then fast, begins to grow. Saying nothing, he draws
thin caricatures – of you – occupies

more and more of all one side of the world
cooling the land as he works. A finger strokes
the field's retreating furrows, knees touch
tree tops, a high head breasts the hill

long before you do. Sooner than expected
the clouds catch fire, send the sun sinking
trailing her warmth as comets might.
The steel moon rises – a cold coin

you aren't ready to spend. Did you see
your shadow race towards her?
How his long arms embraced the night?
How the winter day was no longer light?

Icon Painter

I want to dazzle you
with pigment

fish glue
to swim you towards me –
filling the water with lapis

egg yolk
visions of rings in shop windows

I add rice glue
billions of hearts beating in China
ache with my missing you

egg white
harvest of love from the sheets

They say bone glue and marble
give permanence
my spent flesh is cold with not touching you

Give me some rabbit glue
You lollop over lush fields
faster and faster

How can I catch you?
Bind you in three hundred shades of green?

Gestation

a poem is never finished, only abandoned – Paul Valery

They've moved from one side
of my desk to the other all week

encased in amniotic plastic
sacs from Woolworths

somersaulted through books and papers
wanting to be born

whilst I read around, research, make calls
work on any other thing but …

they kick, asking, just what
am I waiting for?

soon they'll be stunted
starved of air

I need to birth them now
slide them from their smooth wallets

look at them – not like a mother
loving every echo

in their scrunched faces
but coolly, with a nurse's neutrality

snipping umbilici
counting fingers, taking blood, tapping reflexes

and later, when I've watched them
grow a little, let go of their hands

release them to a noisy playground
and retreat, hoping kind children

will invite them to play
that the bullies will leave them in peace.

Pastoral

Deep in the crypt a flock of small children
look up to Canon Peter, his santa-claus cassock,
whiter-than-white beard. They're summer pasture
perpetually moving with the simple impetus
of being young. Wide eyed, docile as lambs

they watch the kind man take a wooden crook
from a glass-fronted cabinet. When he slowly
lowers the curve of its arm round the neck
of the closest boy, their surprised laughter
lifts like small, bright balloons.

He draws the child towards him. *Shepherd! Sheep!* –
elation at knowing the answers. The boy beams
at being caught. They gasp at the crozier's
gleaming brass, shinier than the contents
of any of treasure chest they can imagine –

but don't know *Ivory* and unformed jaws
drop at the thought of elephants
big as cathedrals, for them, more beloved.
The silver chalice awes them. They listen
meek, obedient, still as stooks on a hill.

All the while, the boy's hand lifts
to stroke his own neck still warm
from the embrace of a wooden crook,
the pull of the shepherd.

Going Up-Country

I imagine the end of my life as
being on the London train from Truro
saying farewell to Cornwall's high sky
leaving behind her complicated water
and all the things I couldn't say –
the cathedral still floating
at the head of her river –
three spires pointing the way.

Biographical note

Victoria Field was born in London in 1963. She has lived in Cornwall since 1999 where she works as a writer and poetry therapist. Her first collection is *Olga's Dreams* (fal, 2004) and she has co-edited a textbook on therapeutic writing, *Writing Works*, with Gillie Bolton and Kate Thompson (Jessica Kingsley, 2006). Hall for Cornwall have produced two of her plays, *Blood* (2005) and *Glass Heart* (2006).